CHRISTM

PAVILION
MICHAEL JOSEPH

First published in Great Britain in 1989 by
Pavilion Books Limited
196 Shaftesbury Avenue, London WC2H 8JL
in association with Michael Joseph Limited
27 Wrights Lane, Kensington, London W8 5TZ

Designed by Bridgewater Design Limited

ISBN: 1-85145-376-8

Printed and bound in Singapore by Imago Publishing Limited

10   9   8   7   6   5   4   3   2   1

FOREWORD

*T*he symbols of Christmas are as varied as its origins are complex. The most central is the Nativity, represented by myriad treatments of the Holy Family and the adoration of the baby by the shepherds and kings, and here transferred by Dorothy Hawkesley to surroundings suggestive of the early American settlers. Yet the 25th of December was a pagan festival long before the Christian church adopted it as the birthday of Christ; holly and mistletoe were Druidic fertility symbols; ivy and the yule log also had heathen origins, while the use of the fir as a Christmas tree dates only from Victorian times; and Santa Claus himself derives from St Nicolaus, the patron saint of children, whose feast was traditionally on the 6th of December.

For all that, these archetypal Victorian and Edwardian images of yuletide cheer, with Father Christmas distributing gifts, family entertainments and gatherings around the Christmas tree and the laden dinner table in houses festooned with decorations and presents, as well as wintry outdoor scenes with carol singers, snowmen, sleighrides and tobogganing are images emotive to all of us, none more so than Arthur Rackham's delightful book illustration of Father Christmas and his reindeer threading their way through snowbound streets. They represent the spirit of Christmas – this festive time of gifts and treats, charity and self-indulgence – for believers and non-believers alike all over the world.

FLORENCE HARDY.

FLORENCE HARDY (19th century)
Five Little Girls with Muffs
FAULKNER & CO. LTD., LONDON / BRIDGEMAN ART LIBRARY, LONDON

PUBLISHED BY PAVILION BOOKS LIMITED

FRIEDRICH ORTLIEB (1839-1909)
A Christmas Recital
FINE ART PHOTOGRAPHIC LIBRARY, LONDON

PUBLISHED BY PAVILION BOOKS LIMITED

WILLIAM KRAUSE (1875-1925)
An Alpine Snowscene
N. DRUMMOND / FINE ART PHOTOGRAPHIC LIBRARY, LONDON

PUBLISHED BY PAVILION BOOKS LIMITED

EDWARD FREDERICK BREWTNALL (1846-1902)
Under the Mistletoe
FINE ART PHOTOGRAPHIC LIBRARY, LONDON

PUBLISHED BY PAVILION BOOKS LIMITED

WILLIAM M. SPITTLE (1858-1917)
Glad Tidings
BAUMKOTTER GALLERY / FINE ART PHOTOGRAPHIC LIBRARY, LONDON

PUBLISHED BY PAVILION BOOKS LIMITED

ANON (19th century)
A Jolly Sleighride
FINE ART PHOTOGRAPHIC LIBRARY, LONDON

PUBLISHED BY PAVILION BOOKS LIMITED

A N O N (19th century)
The Christmas Shopping
FINE ART PHOTOGRAPHIC LIBRARY, LONDON

PUBLISHED BY PAVILION BOOKS LIMITED

A N O N (19th century)
Baby's Ride
FINE ART PHOTOGRAPHIC LIBRARY, LONDON

PUBLISHED BY PAVILION BOOKS LIMITED

EDWARD BARNES (active 1856–1882)
The Snowman
CADOGAN GALLERY, LONDON / BRIDGEMAN ART LIBRARY, LONDON

PUBLISHED BY PAVILION BOOKS LIMITED

HUGO MUHLIG (1854-1929)
Hunting in the Snow
JOSEF MENSING GALLERIE, HAMM-RHYNERN/
BRIDGEMAN ART LIBRARY, LONDON

PUBLISHED BY PAVILION BOOKS LIMITED

A N O N (Pears' Print 1896)
Christmas Comes But Once a Year!
FINE ART PHOTOGRAPHIC LIBRARY, LONDON

PUBLISHED BY PAVILION BOOKS LIMITED

GEORGE SHERIDAN KNOWLES (1863-1931)
Christmas
FINE ART PHOTOGRAPHIC LIBRARY, LONDON

PUBLISHED BY PAVILION BOOKS LIMITED

PUBLISHED BY PAVILION BOOKS LIMITED

MARTHA ZEHENTER (19th century)
The Toy Maker
VICTORIA AND ALBERT MUSEUM, LONDON/
BRIDGEMAN ART LIBRARY, LONDON

PUBLISHED BY PAVILION BOOKS LIMITED

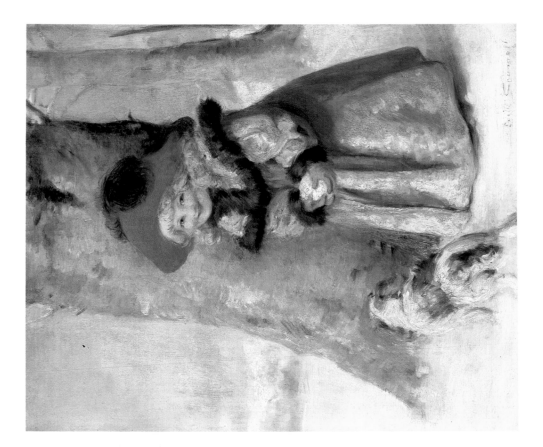

EDITH SCANNELL (active 1880-1921)
Winter Playtime
FINE ART PHOTOGRAPHIC LIBRARY, LONDON

PUBLISHED BY PAVILION BOOKS LIMITED

ROBERT BRAITHWAITE MARTINEAU (1826-69)
The Christmas Hamper
PRIVATE COLLECTION / BRIDGEMAN ART LIBRARY, LONDON

PUBLISHED BY PAVILION BOOKS LIMITED

RALPH PEACOCK (1868-1946)
Christmas Clothes
PHILLIPS, SON AND NEALE, LONDON/
BRIDGEMAN ART LIBRARY, LONDON

PUBLISHED BY PAVILION BOOKS LIMITED

ANON (c.1915)
Children Tobogganing at Christmastime
MARY EVANS PICTURE LIBRARY / JANE DAVAN-WETTON

PUBLISHED BY PAVILION BOOKS LIMITED